DATE DUE

RALPH LAUREN

*Master
of
Fashion*

Anne Canadeo

GEC GARRETT EDUCATIONAL CORPORATION

Cover photo: *Ralph Lauren.* (Cindy Charles/Gamma Liaison.)

Edited and produced by Synthegraphics Corporation

Library of Congress Cataloging in Publication Data

Canadeo, Anne, 1955-
   Ralph Lauren, master of fashion / Anne Canadeo.
      p. cm. — (Wizards of business)
   Includes index.
   Summary: A biography of the man whose early interest in clothes grew and developed into fashion designing for men, women, children, and the home.
   ISBN 1-56074-021-3
   1. Lauren, Ralph—Juvenile literature.   2. Fashion designers—United States—Biography—Juvenile literature.   [1. Lauren, Ralph. 2. Fashion designers.]   I. Title.   II. Series.
TT505.L38C36   1991
746.9'2'092—dc20   91-32777
[B]   CIP
                                                                    AC

Contents

Chronology for **Ralph Lauren**

1939	Born on October 14 in the Bronx, New York
1957	Graduated from DeWitt Clinton High School
1960	Salesman for Mayers Make gloves
1964	Joined A. Rivetz & Company as a tie salesman; married Ricky LowBeer on December 20
1967	Started Polo Fashions as a division of Beau Brummel to make wide ties of his own design
1968	Polo Fashions joined with Norman Hilton to design men's wear
1970	Won first Coty Award for men's wear collection
1971	First independently owned Polo/Ralph Lauren store opened in Beverly Hills, California; designed first women's wear collection
1972	Became sole owner of Polo Fashions
1973	Won second Coty Award; licensed women's wear line
1974	Won third Coty Award
1978	Licensed Ralph Lauren name for perfume line; introduced boy's wear line
1981	Introduced girl's wear line
1983	Introduced Home Collection products
1987	Operated on for a brain tumor

Chapter 1

An Aspiring "Millionaire"

In 1957, Ralph Lauren was about to graduate from DeWitt Clinton High School in the Bronx, a borough of New York City. In the senior class yearbook, the *Clintonian,* the career dreams of each graduate were listed beneath their photograph. Teacher, lawyer, pharmacist were the typical ambitions of Ralph's classmates.

How did Ralph describe his future dreams? Beneath his picture the caption read: "Millionaire."

GROWING UP IN THE BRONX

When Ralph graduated from high school, there was little hint that he would ever achieve his very ambitious goal. He didn't even have a clear idea about the kind of work he would like to do. It certainly wasn't fashion design.

"I didn't know what a fashion designer was in high school,"

Ralph once told Jeffrey Trachtenberg, the author of *Ralph Lauren: The Man Behind the Mystique.* "It was the last thing on my mind."

What was the *first* thing on Ralph's mind? Playing basketball, stickball, or baseball with his friends. He could always find a gang of them in the school yard next door to the apartment house where he lived.

Parents of Opposite Natures

Ralph's family lived in a small, two-bedroom apartment in the Bronx. He was the youngest of four children, born on October 14, 1939. In addition to Ralph there was an older sister, Thelma, and two older brothers, Leonard and Jerome.

Ralph's parents, Frank and Frieda Lifshitz, were both Russian immigrants, but quite opposite in personality. Frank earned a modest living painting houses. He also painted large murals that decorated the lobbies of office buildings in the city.

Frank worked hard to support his family during the difficult years of the **Great Depression.** (Terms in **boldface type** are defined in the Glossary at the back of this book.) But he always dreamed of becoming a famous artist someday whose paintings would hang in museums. He even changed the family name from Lifshitz to Lauren, most likely in the hope that a less foreign-sounding last name would help him sell his paintings.

Everyone in the neighborhood knew Frank Lifshitz. He was very lighthearted and lively in nature, often dressing in a "bohemian" (arty) style. Frieda, on the other hand, was more practical. She was a serious woman and very religious. Like every mother, she wanted her children to succeed in whatever careers they would choose as adults. But it was even more important to Frieda that her children continue to practice the Jewish faith throughout their lifetimes.

The Lifshitz family was very much like other families in the

Bronx neighborhood. Frank and Frieda managed to raise their four children on only fifty to seventy-five dollars a week. Yet, Ralph has remarked that he never felt his family was poor. He considered his family to be like everyone else he knew; struggling to get by, but managing.

Raised with strong religious and family values, Ralph has remained close to his parents, brothers and sisters, and many friends from the Bronx neighborhood. In fact, some later criticized Ralph for allowing old friendships to count too much in his business affairs.

Early Heroes

Although Frank did not make much money, Frieda believed a Jewish education was very important. Until his second year in high school, Ralph attended yeshivas, private Jewish schools. The tuition was costly, but he often received partial scholarships.

At the all-boys school he attended, Ralph had a long day of classes, which included Hebrew and religious studies along with the usual academic subjects. Classes lasted until about six o'clock. Afterward, he would practice basketball for about two hours.

Ralph was an average student. He didn't earn bad grades, but he wasn't at the top of his class either. At the time, he had no interest in art and no obvious artistic skills, like his father. He wanted to be a professional athlete. His heroes were the Yankee home-run hitter, Joe DiMaggio, and basketball players like Bob Cousy of the Boston Celtics.

Basketball was Ralph's favorite sport. He was not very tall (as an adult, he is five feet six inches), but he loved the game and worked hard at it. While a freshman at the Jewish high school he attended for one year, Ralph earned a place on the basketball team. Boyhood friends describe Ralph as "short but aggressive" on the basketball court in those days. "A fast, good player."

A Love of Movies

Ralph has always loved movies. The glamour of Hollywood stars—on and off screen—fascinated him and gave him a glimpse of life beyond the Bronx. The clothes, mannerisms, and personal style of movie characters (or such stars as Katharine Hepburn and Greta Garbo) eventually inspired his clothes designs.

As an established designer, Ralph had the chance to be a part of two Hollywood productions. The first was the film "The Great Gatsby," in 1973, for which he costumed the male actors. The other was the movie "Annie Hall," in 1977, in which he costumed Woody Allen and Diane Keaton. The latter movie started an instant, nationwide trend for women called the "Annie Hall Look."

As a boy, Ralph adored westerns. Randolph Scott, a famous actor of the forties and fifties who often played cowboy roles, was another of Ralph's heroes. Much later, the legends of cowboys and the wild, wide-open West would strongly influence Ralph's clothing and home furnishing designs.

High School Summers

At the end of his freshman year in high school, Ralph persuaded his parents to send him to DeWitt Clinton, an all-boys public high school that was close to where he lived. Ralph had a knack for making friends and was easy to get along with, though sometimes he kept to himself. Friends from high school remember him as being a bit pudgy, and speaking with a slight lisp.

The summer of 1955, before Ralph turned sixteen, he worked as a waiter at Camp Roosevelt, in the Catskill region of upstate New York. It was an important experience for him. He had never really spent much time with people outside of his own familiar neighborhood.

The campers and many of the older counselors at Camp Roosevelt were from more sophisticated and wealthier families than Ralph had ever associated with. He felt like a total outsider, especially since he was a waiter—the lowest rung on the camp "status" ladder. "A waiter was the lowlife of the camp. The rich kids were the campers and you were working," was how Ralph has described it.

Many other teenagers would not have returned to Camp Roosevelt after that first summer. But Ralph did, year after year, eventually working his way up from waiter to head counselor. As Ralph later recalled, "It was a very big thing in my life. I'd started nowhere, at the bottom, not knowing anybody and I worked my way up to being the top counselor. It sounds like nothing now, but at the time it was very important to me."

A PASSION FOR CLOTHES

Dressing well and buying the finest quality clothing were also very important to Ralph in those days. With his father's modest income, he was used to wearing hand-me-downs from his older brothers. But he devised ways to buy his own, new and expensive sweaters or coats as soon as he was able.

From his early teens, Ralph was known for his interest in clothes and his knack for unusual, offbeat outfits. He wasn't afraid to stand out from the crowd by wearing clothes completely different from those of his friends.

His first girl friend, June Ainsworth, met Ralph when she was thirteen and he was fifteen. June has said that Ralph had very "firm" ideas about fashion at that age and about who he was. At the time, he liked traditional "collegiate"- or "preppie"-style clothes— button down, oxford cloth shirts; crew neck sweaters; and camel-colored English-style coats.

It was hard for Ralph to buy the high-priced clothes he liked best. To earn money for the clothes, he worked part time during high school at a department store in his neighborhood and at Camp Roosevelt in the summertime. Somehow, because dressing the way he liked was important to him, he managed to earn enough money to buy the clothes he wanted.

A "Fussy Customer"

Ralph particularly liked traditionally styled clothing. But he often thought the garments needed a little more dash, or extra tailoring. He wanted clothes that were a cross between traditional English styling and the glamour and flair of his favorite Hollywood stars.

Since he couldn't always find what he wanted in the stores, Ralph would have items custom-tailored or even made to order according to his specific directions. Perhaps these made-to-order suits and the painstaking alterations he directed of tailors in men's clothing stores were his very first fashion designs. Did Ralph consider himself an aspiring fashion designer even then? Not at all, he recalls. "Just a very fussy customer."

A BRIEF TRY AT COLLEGE

After graduating from high school in 1957, Ralph wanted to go to college. But because he couldn't afford a private school and his grades were not good enough to win a scholarship, he enrolled at the City College of New York. As a public institution, CCNY was considerably less expensive than other colleges. Ralph attended school part time at night, studying business, and worked part time at department stores during the day.

After two years of this tough schedule, Ralph decided to

leave college. Working in the Bronx and then commuting on the subway to school in Manhattan was tiring, and his grades suffered.

Wanting to work full time, Ralph found a job as a salesman in his favorite store, Brooks Brothers. It was while at Brooks Brothers that he began learning a lot about men's fashions and fabrics. He also learned how to please customers who would pay high prices for personal service and good quality clothes.

Ralph worked at Brooks Brothers for almost six months. Then, because the United States was still drafting men of his age, he served in the Army Reserves for six months at Fort Dix, New Jersey. After the Army, he moved in with his parents again.

FROM MAILROOM TO SALESMAN

Following his stint with the Army, in 1960 Ralph took a job with Mayers Make, a manufacturer of men's and women's gloves. He started off in the back room, packing and mailing gloves according to each salesman's orders.

Ralph's job was a lowly one and his salary was only around fifty dollars a week. But he dressed as if he was making hundreds of dollars a week. Some of the suits he bought cost two hundred dollars, which, compared to today's prices, would be like paying nearly a thousand dollars. His boss, Jerome Fox, had already noticed Ralph's energy and style of dressing. So when Ralph asked for a promotion to salesman, Fox readily agreed.

Thus it was that Ralph Lauren, the twenty-one-year-old aspiring millionaire and dressed in one of his best custom-tailored suits, set out one morning with his box of sample gloves. He was eager to sell the Mayers Make glove **line**, and just as eager to conquer a whole new world—New York City's garment industry.

Chapter 2

Bigger and Better Ties

Ralph sold Mayers Make gloves for about two years, then took another sales position for another glove maker, Daniel Hays, Inc. Because his earnings weren't very high, he also sold a line of perfume to make some extra money. Ralph was a fairly good salesman, but he was always looking for a better opportunity and dreaming about the future.

THE CONSERVATIVE TIE INDUSTRY

After a short while selling gloves for Hays, Ralph took a better-paying job in 1964 as the New York sales representative for A. Rivetz & Company, a Boston tie maker. Rivetz made conservatively styled ties that were sold in stores like Bloomingdale's, Brooks Brothers, and Macy's. Abe Rivetz, the company owner, took a special liking to

Ralph from the start. Rivetz thought the young, flashy-dressed salesman had a special quality and would go far someday.

It was difficult in many ways for Ralph to get along in the tie industry. The salesmen and **buyers** were mostly much older than he and had been working in the same jobs for twenty years or more. Also, the pace was very slow, with buyers taking weeks to make up their minds on orders.

At that time, ties hardly changed at all from year to year. The patterns remained basically the same, with some slight variation in the way the ties were dyed or colored. Sometimes the width might be altered slightly, but usually only by a fraction of an inch.

A Salesman with a Difference

Ralph stood out from the conservative "tie crowd" in many ways. Mainly, however, by the way he dressed. In May 1964, the men's wear industry newspaper, *Daily News Record,* printed a full-page article about Ralph's outstanding wardrobe. The article was titled "The Professional Touch" and contained sketches of a few of Ralph's outfits, including his specially tailored suits and blazers.

Ralph's co-workers at A. Rivetz were shocked by the article and his style of clothing. Abe Rivetz, however, who already knew Ralph was destined for a great future, began copying Ralph's style of dressing and going to Ralph's personal tailor.

Rivetz seemed to be planning a bigger role for Ralph in the company. But he found it very aggravating that Ralph did not drive a sensible car with a trunk that locked, like other salesmen, so that they could carry around the company samples safely.

True to his unique style and taste, Ralph drove a small English sports car. It was a Morgan two-seater that did not have a trunk, only a space behind the front seat, clearly visible through the car windows.

To show Rivetz that he was serious about his commitment to the company, Ralph finally gave in and sold his Morgan. But he still did not buy some stodgy, sensible car like the other salesmen had. His next car was a 1957 Ford Thunderbird, another "flashy" and classic-styled automobile. But it did have a trunk that locked.

LOVE AT FIRST SIGHT

In October of 1963, a few months before joining A. Rivetz, Ralph met Ricky LowBeer, a receptionist at his eye doctor's office. Ricky was nearly six years younger than Ralph and quite attractive. Petite and slim, she had blond hair, blue eyes, and a model's natural good looks.

Ricky's parents were Austrian immigrants, and Ricky also shared Ralph's Jewish faith and upbringing. It was barely six months later when Ralph and Ricky decided to get married. Ralph said later, "It was love at first sight."

Ralph and Ricky were married on December 20, 1964. After a brief honeymoon, they set up housekeeping in a small apartment in the Bronx, just a few blocks from where Ralph's parents lived.

Unfortunately, their happy wedding day was shadowed by sadness for Ralph, for it also brought news that Abe Rivetz had died.

CHANGES AT A. RIVETZ

After the death of Abe Rivetz, the company was run by his son-in-law, Mel Creedman. Ralph did not get along nearly as well with Creedman as he had with Rivetz. When Ralph asked Creedman for the chance to design a new line of ties, Creedman would not give him a clear answer.

Creedman knew Ralph had sophisticated taste and personal style. However, he didn't think Ralph knew what the average person—who made up the bulk of the company's sales—would like to buy in a tie.

Besides, during the early 1960s, ties were not "designed" as they are now. The patterns—widths and shapes—stayed basically the same from year to year. The manufacturers chose fabrics from the few choices offered to them each season by **fabric houses.**

Coloring the Line

Tie manufacturers differed from each other only in the way they colored their line, which meant choosing the colors for backgrounds and stripes, or paisleys. Also, the shades of red, blue, green, yellow, or brown might vary. They could be either bright or subdued.

When Ralph would not take "No" for an answer, Creedman finally allowed him to color the line. But Ralph's first try was a disaster. Phineas Connell, another Rivetz salesman who had been put in charge of overseeing Ralph's color choices, would not approve the designs. Connell thought the colors were much too wild for the customers.

Ralph believed that men were ready for a change in their ties. Nevertheless, he recolored the line, choosing more subdued shades. However, he knew that his colleagues at A. Rivetz & Co. didn't understand him, or what he was trying to do.

The Wide Tie

By 1967 Ralph had been working at A. Rivetz for almost four years. He was taking on more responsibilities in the company and wanted Creedman to listen to his ideas. In Europe, he pointed out, the latest style was wide ties. Not just a fraction of an inch wider, but 3½ to four inches across. The style fascinated Ralph. He had visions of wide ties in exciting colors and unique fabrics—materials that no one had ever thought to use before for a man's tie.

Creedman, however, thought wide ties were ridiculous. Sure, maybe a guy like Ralph, who was dedicated to his wardrobe, would wear such a tie. But the Ralph Laurens of the world were one in ten million. The average A. Rivetz customer would not buy a wide tie.

Thinking "Big"

When Ralph persisted, Creedman finally allowed him to make up a small group of wide ties which Ralph planned to show to Bloomingdale's. If any store would stock such ties, Ralph believed that Bloomingdale's would, since their customers had money and sophisticated, trend-setting tastes.

But Bloomingdale's was not interested in selling the wide ties. Ralph still believed, however, that sooner or later, the prestigious store would want such ties. He believed, too, that all the better stores would eventually want the wide ties that he could design.

MOVING ON

Ralph also knew that he wouldn't be designing wide ties for A. Rivetz. He decided it was time to start his own tie company. However, he was only a twenty-six-year-old salesman who some people in the industry thought was inexperienced and untried. Moreover, he certainly didn't have the money to start a new company.

But Ralph was determined. He believed he had a product that people would buy. If only he could find someone who shared that belief with him.

Chapter 3

The Start of Polo Fashions

During the winter and spring of 1967, Ralph approached many potential **financial backers,** telling them about his vision of wide, wonderful ties. Some were not interested. Others were interested but were not willing to risk their money on such a gamble. Then Ralph met Ned Brower, the president of Beau Brummel, a tie company based in Cincinnati, Ohio.

A CHANGING INDUSTRY

Brower agreed with Ralph that the men's wear industry was changing. Several famous designers of women's wear, such as Pierre Cardin and Bill Blass, were now putting their names on men's wear lines through **licensing agreements.**

Traditionally, manufacturers of men's wear gave no credit to individual designers. They weren't even called designers, but were referred to as tailors or stylists. However, the new trend of designer recognition suggested that men were becoming more aware of designers by name, and perhaps would shop by designer name rather than by maker name. This was the practice in the women's wear market.

The trend toward the use of a designer's name also suggested that men were becoming more style conscious. As a result, men's styles would be more varied and have more obvious changes from season to season, just like women's fashions.

Taking a Gamble

But would men pay more for outlandishly styled ties? Brower looked at the trends in men's wear and decided that they would. He already ran a profitable, thriving company that made a conservative, standard line of ties. Ralph's ties would not overlap with his established line and could be a valuable addition to the company, Brower reasoned. If the line failed, the losses would not be too great.

BEAU BRUMMEL'S NEW DIVISION

In April of 1967, Ralph joined Beau Brummel as the head of the company's new division, created specifically to manufacture and sell his wide ties.

Ralph wasn't sure what to call the new division, which was set up as a separate company. Then his brother Jerry came up with the idea of using the word "polo." Polo was a sport played mainly by millionaires and royalty, like Prince Charles of England. The word brought to mind an entire picture of rolling, green estates, country mansions, aristocratic players, and well-dressed spectators.

Ralph thought the word would appeal to the kind of customers he hoped to attract. These were people who set a high priority on stylish, quality clothes and were willing to spend extra money for them. Following brother Jerry's suggestion, Ralph named his new company Polo Fashions.

The first office of Polo Fashions was in the Empire State Building, on 34th Street in New York City. It was a small, back room of Beau Brummel's New York office. Ralph had no window, and kept his sample ties in a drawer of his desk. In six months, he was able to move into a slightly larger room, where he at least had a chest of drawers in which to store his ties.

A One-Man Show

Ralph finally had his own company. He was the president and the only employee. Whatever job had to be done, it was up to Ralph to do it.

Just as he had always dreamed, Ralph could now design the kinds of ties he had always wanted. He chose bold, block-printed fabrics with bright colors as well as unique fabrics that he found in remnant stores. He found the perfect tailor, George Bruder, to make the ties to his specific directions. Ralph sometimes fussed over the smallest of details, but Bruder liked him and had a lot of patience.

To sell his ties, Ralph visited shop after shop of men's wear stores. And he met with all the big department store buyers. The line was also sold by other Beau Brummel salesmen, but only if they had time after selling the company's regular products. In addition to being the top salesman for Polo Fashions, Ralph also kept all financial records and personally packed and shipped all orders.

Accounts: Few but "Special"

His first six months in business, Ralph sold his ties to barely two dozen accounts. The ties were very different from anything that buyers in the men's wear departments of big stores had ever seen before. The look of the ties alone was enough to scare most buyers off.

However, even if they liked them, buyers were turned off when they realized that the ties had to be priced at ten to fifteen dollars each. The average price of a tie at the time was three to five dollars. Nobody would pay more for a tie, they complained.

Ralph pointed out the quality of the fabrics, the special hand-sewn construction, and the uniqueness of his ties. Each one was practically an individual work of art. Tie buyers might agree with that point, but they still did not place any orders.

But Ralph did manage to sell his ties to Roland Meledandri, an exclusive men's store whose name had a lot of status when he mentioned it to other potential customers. Also, he sold the ties to Paul Stuart, a store in which he had purchased many of his own clothes. The Paul Stuart name also impressed other customers.

Although his ties were not exactly setting the world of men's wear on fire, Ralph was not discouraged. He was optimistic and persistent, determined to build on his small successes.

"The Idea Behind the Look"

The *Daily News Record* took notice of Ralph once more and wrote a favorable piece about his latest venture. "I'm promoting a level of taste, a total feeling," the article quoted the young tie designer. "It's important to show the customer how to wear these ties, the idea behind the look."

Perhaps all fashion designers were selling a particular "idea behind the look," but only Ralph managed to state that objective quite so specifically. As his work as a designer later expanded to other men's wear as well as women's wear and decorative items for the home, Ralph's objective of selling the customer an idea—even a complete fantasy—behind his styles would remain constant.

A Persistent, Persuasive Promoter

With no money for advertising, Ralph had to think of innovative ways to build a reputation for his ties, with consumers and within the men's wear industry. He was soft-spoken at times, and many have described him as humble. But Ralph was persistent and could be a showman when he needed to step into the spotlight. He also had a gift for seeking out important and influential supporters.

For example, Ralph knew that Henry Grethel's interest in his ties could help Polo Fashions considerably. Grethel was a successful designer of shirts for Hathaway, a major manufacturer of men's shirts.

Ralph knew that customers often asked for the same ties they saw in the Hathaway magazine ads that featured Grethel shirts. Grethel chose the ties himself, and tie manufacturers competed for the chance to have their products in Hathaway ads.

Ralph arranged for a personal appointment with Grethel, and much to his surprise, Grethel liked the ties. Grethel had already promised other tie makers that he would use their ties in ads showing his new shirt designs. But Ralph was so persuasive that Grethel decided to use the striking, wide ties from Polo instead.

Grethel turned out to be one of Ralph's earliest and most influential supporters. He introduced Ralph to many important buyers for **retail** stores. However, the big retail stores, like Bloomingdale's and Saks Fifth Avenue, were not quite ready for Ralph's ties. But this only meant that Ralph had to try even harder.

In the meantime, Ralph's client list of small men's stores was growing. It included the Eric Ross men's shop in Beverly Hills and Louis of Boston. All were exclusive stores that catered to very wealthy customers.

Ralph also contacted fashion editors at magazines and newspapers. He spent hours cultivating their interest—talking on the phone and meeting at lunches, or showing his ties wherever and whenever people would agree to see them. He was a relentless and persistent promoter.

Ralph's efforts finally paid off when Bob Green, fashion editor at the popular men's magazine, *Playboy,* agreed to use Ralph's ties in a magazine feature on men's fashions. The photo layout included styles by designers Bill Blass and Pierre Cardin. Although a newcomer in the fashion industry, Ralph was already beginning to rub shoulders with the big design stars.

AN OFFER FROM BLOOMINGDALE'S

Ever since starting his own company—and even while he was still at A. Rivetz—Ralph had been trying to get Bloomingdale's interested in his wide ties.

Gary Schafer, who was in charge of buying ties for the store, also designed ties for Bloomingdale's own store label, Sutton East. Bloomingdale's did not believe in promoting individual designers, Ralph was told. The only designer label they carried in the men's department was that of the classic French designer, Christian Dior. They were not about to break their rule for a newcomer and a nobody.

But Schafer finally made Ralph an offer. He would buy Ralph's ties on two conditions: if the ties were made narrower by at least an inch and if the Polo label was taken off and Bloomingdale's own label put on instead.

As much as Ralph wanted his ties in Bloomingdale's, he said, "No deal." Ned Brower, the president of Beau Brummel and the owner of Polo Fashions, didn't understand. He thought Ralph was making a mistake. The fledgling company needed money. Once Bloomingdale's sold the ties, other department stores would want them, too. Didn't Ralph want to make money?

Of course he did. But if the ties were made narrower and sold with Bloomingdale's label in them, Ralph thought he would lose everything that made his ties distinctive, different, and unique.

Ralph was sure that, sooner or later, Bloomingdale's would buy his ties, without any alterations and with the Polo label inside.

The Doors Finally Open

Ralph was right. A few months later, Schafer's assistant, Steve Krauss, was promoted to head of the men's department at Bloomingdale's in Fresh Meadows, a suburb of New York City. Krauss had always liked Ralph's ties, and in the spring of 1968 he put them in his men's department.

The ties were an instant smash hit with shoppers. Krauss could not believe that people were willing to pay so much so quickly for a tie, but there was no arguing with success.

Soon after, Bloomingdale's main store in the city stocked Ralph's ties in a special display for Father's Day, June 1968. Ralph went to the store and polished the four-foot glass showcase himself.

It was an important moment for Ralph. He had done what he had set out to do, without compromising the style of his ties. The doors to Bloomingdale's had finally opened for Polo Fashions. It would turn out to be an important and profitable relationship for both the store and the fashion house.

In 1989, Ralph Lauren donated funds for 15 computers and a satellite hookup to the Ridgway School, which is located near his ranch in Colorado, because the students were so isolated from other schools. (Polo/Ralph Lauren.)

PROTECTING THE EXCLUSIVE MYSTIQUE

After being in business for a year and doing rather well, Ralph still was not selling large volumes of his ties. So Ned Brower was quite surprised and very displeased when he heard that Ralph had turned away another big customer.

This time the customer was Wallach's, a chain of men's stores that had wanted to order the ties, but Ralph refused to take the order. He didn't think the chain had the right stylish image for his ties, or attracted customers who would pay the price for his product.

Ralph also thought that putting the ties in a chain store would ruin the product's image of exclusivity. If a person pays a lot of money for a product they think is unique, he believed, they don't want to see that product in every store in town. He thought people would think that the ties were less valuable if they became too common and easily available.

Looking back, Ralph's refusal to sell ties to Wallach's didn't seem to hurt Polo Fashions' eventual success. At the time, however, Brower thought the decision was a serious mistake and perhaps showed that Ralph did not have good business judgment.

Chapter 4

Polo Fashions Rides On

A year after joining Beau Brummel, Ralph's persistence was paying off. His ties were gaining a "wide" reputation and orders were increasing. In April of 1968, he was interviewed again by the *Daily News Record* and spoke of even more ambitious goals. "My long-range wish would be to design all kinds of men's wear, not just ties."

Just about that time, Ralph received a call from a man named Norman Hilton, a very well-known maker of men's suits. Hilton's suits were sold in such fine stores as Saks Fifth Avenue and Jordan Marsh.

Hilton had a keen eye for new trends in men's wear. He couldn't help but notice that, suddenly, the latest rage among fashion-conscious friends was Polo Fashions' outrageous, wide ties. He had to know who was making them and finally found out it was Ralph Lauren.

A NEW VENTURE

When Hilton met with Ralph, he proposed that the young designer join Hilton's company. He wanted Ralph to design ties for his line of suits so that the firm could offer a total look. This might have sounded like a good deal to another fledgling designer in Ralph's position. Hilton was a very large, well-established firm, and the deal would be a profitable one.

But Ralph refused Hilton's offer and then made one of his own. He wasn't interested in working for anyone else. He agreed that putting together a total look in men's wear—a line that included ties, suits, jackets, casual wear, coats, and the like—was a great idea. But just as he had told the *Daily News Record,* Ralph wanted to design it all, not only the ties. Ralph added that he would consider being partners with Hilton in such a venture.

Now it was Hilton's turn to refuse. But several months later, the two finally came to an agreement. Ralph and Hilton entered into a partnership in which Hilton's company would make the suits and other men's wear garments that Ralph was so eager to design.

The Move to Men's Wear

Ralph and Brower were able to come to a quick agreement when Ralph decided it was now time for Polo Fashions to leave Beau Brummel. He was even able to take the name Polo Fashions and the Polo **trademark** (a polo player on horseback) for his own.

Ralph moved the Polo offices to a midtown Manhattan location, just west of Fifth Avenue on 55th Street. It was not the typical location for a fashion house, although fashion designer John Weitz had a showroom there. But most fashion-related businesses were located a bit farther downtown, on the West Side, in an area of the city known as "the garment district."

Ralph didn't want to be in a big garment-district building, where he was one of a thousand names on the listing in the lobby. It was important for him to maintain an image of individuality and exclusivity, for his company and its products.

The First Show

On October 22, 1968, Ralph's first men's suit design was shown to the public at a fashion show in the Plaza Hotel. Other designers who presented new designs included such famous names as John Weitz, Oleg Cassini, Bill Blass, and Pierre Cardin. Ralph was just starting out, but already he was playing on the same field as "major league stars."

At the new offices, Ralph expanded his staff. He hired Steve Krauss, who had gone around other executives at Bloomingdale's in order to buy Ralph's ties.

In October of 1969, Polo Fashions showed its first collection, men's fashions for the spring of 1970. The clothes could generally be described as classic styles, made with high-quality fabrics such as fine linen and white flannel.

To these traditional styles, Ralph always introduced a new touch—a slightly different cut in a jacket, pleats in trousers, wider lapels. He gave a fresh interpretation to conservative, classic styles. Looking back, some fashion experts would say that in this first collection, Ralph had shown the course he would follow for many years to come.

Problems with Being Understood

However, there was more to putting out an entire men's wear line than Ralph had ever expected. Unlike most other designers, he had never attended design school and did not have many of the necessary technical skills, such as sketching, **draping,** and **pattern making.** He knew how he wanted a suit to look, but he did not know exactly how it was to be constructed, from start to finish. Often, he didn't realize that some of his ideas broke the basic rules of tailoring.

Perhaps his lack of technical skills made Ralph's ideas more exciting and unique than those of many other designers. But in those early days of the Hilton-Lauren partnership, the problems that Ralph created in the factory were very frustrating for everyone involved. But the most frustrated of all was Michael Cifarelli, a tailor, pattern maker, and the head of Hilton's suit factory.

It was up to Cifarelli to interpret Ralph's explanations of how he wanted his designs to look. Their meetings became very heated at times. Cifarelli was a master tailor and known throughout the business for his fine workmanship, but he could not seem to understand Ralph's ideas about men's suits. Once, while Ralph was pointing out the problems with a suit jacket on a factory dummy, Cifarelli tore the jacket off the dummy and stomped up and down on it in total frustration.

A Total Disaster

There is an old saying that a giraffe was designed by a committee. It means that when too many people become involved in designing something, it's bound to turn out badly. After Ralph's first shipment of suits were sent out from Hilton's factory, some shoppers thought that the same group who had designed the giraffe had also designed these suits!

Some problems were actually funny: pants with legs that were too long, jackets with arms that were too short. At the time, Ralph didn't think it was a very laughable matter. Neither did Norman Hilton when Bloomingdale's sent its entire shipment back. But Hilton had patience and wanted his partnership with Ralph to work. He knew Ralph was talented, but needed to learn more of the basics about men's wear design and manufacturing.

Another Failure— and Fatherhood

After the first suits were returned, Ralph made another fashion miscalculation. This time, the problem was not bad measurements. Ralph returned from a business trip to Europe with the idea of what he called an "unconstructed" look to men's suits and jackets. He designed some blazers and suits, modeling them after the unlined, form-fitting cloth jackets that are worn by many waiters.

Some fashion editors liked the look, but at the time, shoppers did not. It was another disappointment for Ralph, but he did not give up. Years later, the same basic idea of unconstructed, unlined suits and blazers became very popular, for both men and women.

Although Ralph's first year in men's wear was marked by ups and downs, the spring of 1969 brought happy news. Ralph and Ricky had already moved from the Bronx to an apartment on Manhattan's upper East Side. On May 7, their first child, Andrew, was born. Ralph Lauren, fashion designer, was now a father. The importance of family had been taught to him by his own parents, and he took fatherhood seriously.

Meeting a Gifted Tailor

Despite his first failures, Ralph still believed in his ideas about innovative fashions for men. He knew that the problem was not with his designs, but with the process of getting those designs produced. Faced with this problem, it was a lucky day when Ralph met a master tailor named Leo Lozzi.

Lozzi was a partner in Lantham Clothes, a men's wear company in Lawrence, Massachusetts. When Ralph visited his factory, Lozzi showed Ralph a jacket he had just made. Ralph saw instantly that this was the man who could successfully interpret his ideas. By July of 1970, Ralph had moved the production of his clothes from Hilton's factory in New Jersey to the Lantham factory in Massachusetts.

Lozzi once described how Ralph explained his ideas about a design for a suit jacket: " . . . he made gestures with his hands . . . rounder, softer, a longer lapel, high pockets . . . I understood what he wanted."

THE FIRST COTY AWARD

Each year, members of the fashion world assemble for the presentation of the Coty Awards. The first Coty for men's fashions had been awarded in 1969, to Bill Blass. Unbelievably, the next Coty Award,

THE COTY AWARD

The Coty American Fashion Critics' Award was started in 1943 by Eleanor Lambert, who worked for Coty Cosmetics. She thought that sponsoring a fashion award would make the cosmetics company appear more prestigious.

The Coty Award became the clothing industry's own Academy Award. Until 1969, however, awards were only given to designers of women's fashions. Prior to the 1960s, the men's wear industry did not use the word "designer" to describe the men or women who worked behind the scenes in a men's wear factory as master tailors or stylists.

But in the 1960s, all that changed as many famous designers of women's wear—such as Bill Blass and Pierre Cardin—began designing men's fashions. To keep up with these changes, the Coty Award added a new prize for men's wear designer in 1969, and the first recipient was Bill Blass.

for best men's wear designer of 1970, went to Ralph Lauren. It was no surprise, however, that the award followed soon after Ralph began to work with the gifted "interpretor," Leo Lozzi.

Despite some setbacks, Ralph was now firmly established as a full-fledged designer and a rising star in the men's wear industry.

Chapter 5

The Polo Player Scores Again

Winning the Coty Award was a big boost to Ralph's reputation. It helped him persuade Bloomingdale's to give his men's wear line it's own special space, or what he called a designer "shop."

A SHOP IN A STORE

Ralph claimed that in order to show his line to its best advantage, all of his clothes—suits, shirts, pants, and sportswear—as well as matching accessories that were made abroad, such as belts and luggage, needed to be displayed in one special space within the store. He was not just trying to sell a tie at one counter and a shirt at another, but an entire image—a complete wardrobe that was carefully planned out by the designer.

Ralph reasoned that a man who bought a Ralph Lauren suit for the daytime would also want ties, shirts, and even a top coat of similar design and quality. When the workday was over, that same customer would want to change into Polo sportswear for home and the weekends. Ralph wanted all of these clothes to be easily available to the shopper, in one location in a store.

Also, since he still had little money for advertising, an in-store shop would be the best way to promote his **merchandise** to customers.

Bloomingdale's First Men's Designer Shop

At first, Bloomingdale's brushed off the idea of a Ralph Lauren shop. They insisted that the store couldn't give an individual designer his own **boutique** in the men's department, even though this was done to some degree in women's wear. But when Ralph threatened to find another store willing to give him what he wanted, Bloomingdale's agreed to his request.

Ralph also knew exactly how he wanted the shop to look. He wanted the space to be decorated in a way that suggested an English country house—wood paneling with oriental rugs and antique furniture. He wanted the shop to look classy, but not stuffy. He imagined that this was the kind of place his typical customers aspired to or fantasized about living in. The atmosphere of the shop suggested a monied, upper-class world in which he believed shoppers wanted to share.

In the fall of 1971, the Ralph Lauren shop opened in Bloomingdale's. Once again, despite the critics, the shop idea was a great success. It is now very common to see designers' shops in both men's and women's departments of large stores. But the idea was brand new at the time.

THE SUCCESSFUL LIFE

The Bloomingdale's shop was not the only exciting event for the Lauren family in the fall of 1971. On October 3, their second son, David, was born. By now, they had moved from the one-bedroom apartment on New York's fashionable upper East Side to a two-bedroom apartment in the same building.

At age thirty-two, Ralph was a very young and successful **entrepreneur** who owned half of a company that was doing nearly four million dollars a year in sales. Polo's profits for 1971 were about $299,000.

The Laurens were an active young couple who enjoyed their two children, sports, and the outdoors. One of Ralph's great passions had always been expensive, classic cars. (He even keeps a collection of prized miniatures of his favorite models in his office.) Now he was able to indulge his tastes by buying a silver Mercedes sedan. He and Ricky also enjoyed racing a Jeep along the ocean shoreline during summers at the Hamptons, a favorite vacation spot on Long Island for wealthy New Yorkers.

Many consider the Laurens friendly and personable, but quite private. Unlike many other big names in the fashion industry, Ralph and Ricky do not participate much in New York night life— charity balls, society parties and the like. However, they are involved in several charity efforts, including cancer research, raising funds for needy children, and supporting the New York City AIDS Fund.

When Ralph isn't working, he likes to spend time with his family in a private setting, such as their New York apartment or at one of their many vacation homes. He has continued to remain close to his parents, brothers, and sister.

Ralph is also loyal to old friends he had grown up with. Many, including his brother Lenny, have become involved in his business over the years. This has sometimes worked out well and sometimes it hasn't, for Ralph or his friends. Still, he continues to put loyalty above business "rules."

POLO ON RODEO DRIVE

Soon after the Ralph Lauren shop opened in Bloomingdale's, Jerry Magnin approached Ralph with a new idea. Magnin was the grandson of Joseph Magnin, who had founded the Magnin department stores. Jerry Magnin had a shop in Beverly Hills, California, on the exclusive shopping thoroughfare known as Rodeo Drive, a street with some of the world's most expensive stores.

Magnin wanted to carry Ralph's complete line in his store. But because Polo Fashions already had an agreement that only one store in Southern California could carry their products, they could not sell their line to Magnin.

Then Magnin came up with an even more tempting proposition. What if he opened an entire store on Rodeo Drive that stocked and sold only Ralph Lauren's men's wear? The Ralph Lauren name would be above the door, and Magnin would build the store and decorate it exactly as Ralph wanted. Would Polo Fashions be interested in that idea?

Despite Polo's previous agreement with another store in the area, Ralph was certainly interested in Magnin's new idea. Berny Schwartz, the owner of the other store with whom Polo had an agreement, would not sell Polo suits. This was partly because of design problems and partly because Schwartz wanted to showcase his own brand of suits. When the agreement with Schwartz was finally dissolved, Schwartz felt that he had not been treated fairly. Nevertheless, the Ralph Lauren store on Rodeo Drive opened without a legal dispute.

Ironing Out Some Wrinkles

The Rodeo Drive store opened in September of 1971. As Magnin had promised, the shop was good advertising for the Ralph Lauren name and added status to the label. It was successful for the first few months, but then problems began to occur.

The biggest problem was a lack of **stock.** The shelves were often empty because they held only Ralph Lauren merchandise (except for items he had not yet designed, such as shoes). The need to put more items in the store pushed Ralph into new areas, such as designing shoes, belts, and sweaters.

There were also delivery problems. Frequently the store would get items much too late for them to be of interest to customers, such as winter sweaters in May. This same problem existed at other stores that also sold Polo items and came back to haunt the firm months later.

At the time, the delivery problem was a disaster for the Rodeo Drive store. If they didn't receive merchandise, they didn't have anything to sell. All problems were eventually corrected, but they did reduce the store's first-year sales.

In addition to the store in Beverly Hills, there are now over sixty independently owned Ralph Lauren stores in the United States. They sell over $150 million worth of clothes and home products a year. As part of Ralph Lauren's global expansion in the 1980s, independently owned stores were opened in seventeen countries worldwide. By 1991, worldwide retail sales (including department, specialty, and Polo stores) for all Polo/Ralph Lauren products were approximately three billion dollars.

GOING IN REVERSE

Around the time the Rodeo Drive store was opened, Ralph was persuaded to design blouses for women. It's said that a female department store executive who ordered Ralph's men's shirts for her store kept asking the Polo salesman when Ralph was going to design some decent shirts for women.

"Never," Ralph said at first. He had no interest in entering women's wear. His men's wear line was just getting off the ground. Well-known fashion designers of women's clothes often moved into men's wear—such as Bill Blass and Pierre Cardin—but never in reverse. Nobody thought such a move could be successful. Women shoppers would not be interested in buying fashions from a men's wear designer, no matter who he was.

But after much persuasion, Ralph Lauren proved otherwise. He designed women's shirts in a tailored style, to look like men's shirts, and used high-quality cotton, linen, and silk. Instead of using the standard Polo Fashions label inside the shirts, Ralph changed the label to read, "Polo by Ralph Lauren." He thought it would add a more personal touch that would appeal to women shoppers.

A New Status Symbol

Another personal touch that Ralph gave to the women's shirts was the addition of the company's polo player **logo** on the shirt cuff. It was a small detail, barely an inch long. But the addition of the polo player logo eventually turned out to be a **marketing** brainstorm. The emblem became a status symbol for women. It sent a message to the world that the woman wearing a Ralph Lauren blouse had taste, style, and financial success. Ralph was one of the first designers to use a logo as a marketing tool.

While models wait to go on stage, Ralph Lauren peeks nervously at the audience to see how people are reacting to his new designs. (Gamma Liaison.)

An Instant Success

The women's blouses, first sold in Bloomingdale's, were an instant success. Bloomingdale's asked for an exclusive right to the new Polo merchandise and opened another in-store Ralph Lauren shop for the women's shirts.

One problem with the shirts, however, was the fit. Because Ralph refused to hire a **fitting model,** the blouses were not designed for a "standard"-size female body. Instead, Ralph chose to use his design assistant for his model. But because she was slim and small proportioned, the blouses were not cut to fit the average woman's figure properly.

Ralph was told of this problem by his sales manager and by department store executives, but it didn't seem to bother him. Some people said he only cared if his blouse designs looked good on his wife, Ricky. And fortunately for her, like the model Ralph used, she was also trim and petite.

Most women, however, had to buy Ralph's blouses a size or more larger than they usually needed in order for the buttons to close properly and the sleeves to be the correct length. But this inconvenience didn't stop women from taking part in the latest, chic fashion trend.

POLO'S FIRST WOMEN'S WEAR LINE

The success of his blouses quickly convinced Ralph to design other fashions for women. His first women's wear collection was presented to the industry in 1971. According to the company's own description, the clothes were designed for a woman "who is active, independent, and assured."

Ralph's designs were influenced by Hollywood's "glamour" actresses of the 1930s and 1940s. According to a company statement at the time, his clothes were designed for women who might have the same taste or personal style as movie stars like Katharine Hepburn or Greta Garbo.

Katharine Hepburn was famous for her tailored, "sporty" wardrobe of loose-fitting but elegant clothes. She was usually photographed wearing pants and tweedy blazers, when most other actresses were modeling sequined evening gowns.

Hepburn's clothes and personality projected the image of an

independent, active woman who also had an upper-class background and classic "Yankee" values. This was perhaps a large part of the ideal woman Ralph Lauren was trying to create with his fashion designs.

Ralph seemed to believe that many women would prefer to wear men's tailored clothing, but altered to fit a female figure. Over the years, his range of designs for women has varied widely, but this basic principle seems to remain constant.

MEN'S WEAR AND WOMEN'S WEAR: A BIG DIFFERENCE

As Ralph's company expanded into women's wear, it met with great success. But the company also learned that women's wear is vastly different from men's wear. The pace is much faster, since it is necessary to design women's clothes for many more seasons than men's clothes.

Each year, new women's clothing designs are needed for spring, summer, fall, and holiday-resort wear in winter. The work required to design and manufacture a season's collection is monumental. Creating new sketches, devising patterns, and choosing fabrics are only a small part of the process.

Also, manufacturing and shipping orders on time are critically important for any clothing maker. As Ralph's company expanded into the more demanding area of women's wear, the problems of manufacturing and distribution became greater and greater.

Chapter 6

A Financial Time Bomb

At the time that Ralph entered the women's wear market, his company was doing about four million dollars a year in sales. It owned a men's shirt factory in Mount Vernon, just north of New York City, sold a full line of high-priced men's wear, and had created a second, moderate-priced line of men's wear that was sold under the Chaps label.

STORM CLOUDS AHEAD

Despite the company's obvious success, Ralph saw storm clouds gathering in the not too distant future for his firm. He realized that he did not have the business skills necessary to manage such a varied and rapidly growing operation.

Ralph had immense talent as a designer and keen instincts for marketing. He also had terrific persistence and a great deal of luck. But he was the first to admit he was totally self-taught when it came to the financial aspects of managing a growing business.

Calling on a Friend for Help

In 1971, Ralph was faced with mounting problems at Polo that ranged from delivery and manufacturing delays to difficulties with loan arrangements. He turned to Michael Bernstein, who Ralph had grown up with in his old Bronx neighborhood.

Bernstein was a successful certified public accountant who handled many businesses in the garment industry. Polo was one of his accounts. Ralph was impressed with his old friend's financial skills and worked hard to persuade Bernstein to join Polo.

Bernstein finally agreed and joined the firm in May of 1971. He saw a good future in the growing company and thought he could solve its present problems. The first day on the job he was faced with his first crisis—a payment of $300,000 was due on a loan from a Boston bank. It was certainly more money than the company could possibly pay back on such short notice.

Bernstein calmly tried to convince the bank that Polo was a healthy, growing company and would soon be able to pay back the debt. To prove this, he had to show the bank sales figures and projections of the company's growth for the coming months. Most well-organized companies have systems to account for production and sales figures, and a means of controlling inventory. At the time, Polo's systems—what there were—were haphazard and its figures inaccurate.

As Bernstein labored to put together profit projection figures for the bank, he began to realize that Polo was more disorganized than he had suspected.

Problems with Returns

The bank was also concerned about the high returns of Polo goods from department stores. If Polo shipped 1,000 pairs of pants to a store and they arrived damaged, the store would return the pants to Polo without paying for them. Sometimes the clothes would not be damaged, but would arrive too late for the season, such as spring linen suits delivered in July.

When Bernstein arrived at Polo, he found that up to thirteen percent of all merchandise the firm shipped came back. The industry average was more like three to six percent.

Many people blamed the problem of late deliveries on Ralph's detail-minded and perfectionist tendencies. He would delay production until he was absolutely satisfied with every thread of a new design. He never knew when to just stop fussing and let a design go into production, some said. He couldn't get out of his own way.

The bankers appreciated quality clothing. But they didn't like lending money on the basis of 1,000 suits being sold and then learning later that those suits were returned to Polo—unsold— because they were delivered too late.

Collection Problems

Another money problem plaguing Polo was in collecting payments owed to the company. Ralph had avoided putting his clothes in too many big department stores because he thought it would ruin the image of exclusivity. Therefore, many of his accounts were small boutiques.

The shoppers were wealthy, but the boutique owners often ran their stores on a small margin of profit. Suppliers like Polo were sometimes last on the list of those to be paid at the end of a month.

Ralph liked having his clothes in these small stores. He would keep sending merchandise even if old bills hadn't been paid. However, this left Polo with a gap of tens of thousands of dollars that was owed to the firm.

"Buying Out" Norman Hilton

Although Bernstein worked hard to straighten things out, financial, production, and delivery problems continued to plague the firm. Part of the difficulty was because he did not get cooperation from many employees who had been with Ralph for a long time and now resented Bernstein as a "newcomer."

Also, the company continued to grow at a phenomenal rate. Sales increased from four million dollars in 1971 to nearly eight million dollars in 1972. Efforts to gain control of the disorganized manufacturing, shipping, and billing systems could not keep up with the rapid growth.

At the same time, Ralph decided that he no longer wanted Norman Hilton as a partner. Hilton still owned half of the company, even though the clothes were not made in the Hilton factory and he took little part in the actual running of the business.

After nearly a year of negotiation, Hilton agreed in December of 1972 to sell his half of the firm to Ralph for $633,000. The company was booking more and more orders every day. But after paying manufacturing costs, salaries, and other expenses, there was so little money left that Ralph had to borrow $150,000 to make his first payment to Hilton.

Bernstein was now having trouble finding new banks and **factors** willing to loan money to the company. Although the firm's designs were award winners and the clothes were amazingly successful with consumers, poor financial management was a slow time bomb, ticking away and about to explode.

The only one who didn't hear it ticking seemed to be Ralph Lauren.

THE BOMB EXPLODES

In March of 1973, the many financial problems at Polo came to a head. The year before, Polo had taken more orders than it could fill, and shipped out too much of its merchandise too late. The company also owed Hilton $500,000, due in quarterly payments.

The firm's factor, J.P. Maguire, was becoming very worried about its investment in Polo. The company owed over $500,000 to financial backers and suppliers. Ralph handed over his personal bank book, with a balance of $100,000, as **collateral.** Maguire sent David Goldberg to figure out Polo's bookkeeping. Goldberg found that Polo was owed over half a million dollars by stores who wouldn't or couldn't pay their bills.

Ralph had wanted to be the sole owner of the firm very badly. But now he thought that buying out Hilton had been a mistake, or at least poor timing. He blamed Bernstein for poor advice on the decision.

Then it was discovered by Maguire's staff that the Chaps division of Polo had lost $200,000 in 1972. Bernstein was blamed again and fired.

On the recommendation of Goldberg, Ralph hired Harvey Hellman to take on the tremendous task of untangling Polo's bookkeeping.

An Uphill Climb

It was a hard, uphill battle in 1973 for Ralph to keep Polo going. The firm might get a million-dollar order from Bloomingdale's, but there was not enough cash on hand to buy supplies and manufacture the goods.

Ralph was forced to lay off many employees, and many others quit, afraid that the company was going out of business. The gossip about Polo around the garment district predicted the worst.

A Way Out of the Problems

Goldberg came up with a four-point plan to keep Ralph in business. The first was licensing the women's wear line. In October of 1973, Ralph signed a ten-year licensing agreement with Stuart Kreisler. Polo would receive $250,000 as a licensing fee and five to seven percent of yearly sales. Ralph would continue to design the women's clothing, but Kreisler would buy fabric, then manufacture and ship the products. This left Polo free to concentrate on the men's wear line.

The $250,000 licensing fee from Stuart Kreisler gave Ralph more **capital** to invest in the business, which was the second point of Goldberg's plan. The third point was working out an extended payback schedule of the debt to Hilton. The fourth was working out another extended payback schedule on $500,000 that Polo owed to the clothing company that made its men's suits.

Ralph, with the help of Hellman and Goldberg, managed to accomplish all parts of Goldberg's plan. Stumbling along, the embattled polo player managed to make it through another year of business.

In 1973, Ralph also won his second Coty Award for his men's wear designs.

The Last Crisis

Most people closely involved in Polo's troubles thought that the company was now on the road to recovery. But J.P. Maguire, Polo's factor, disagreed.

Another crisis hit when Maguire sent word to Polo that its financial backing would be withdrawn in sixty days. Some thought this would be the death blow for the company. But Polo was able to find United Virginia Factoring Company as a new factor.

Polo continued to operate, using better systems and paying back creditors on time. The firm also licensed out another division, Chaps men's wear, which helped reduce costs even further. By the spring of 1974, the company had clearly survived all crises and was on financially stable ground.

In the summer of 1974, Ralph proudly accepted his third Coty Award, this time for his women's designs. This award meant a great deal to him. Despite the dark days of near **bankruptcy,** the award affirmed Ralph's survival and talent. He was also now able to move his family into a beautiful apartment on Fifth Avenue, in a building that overlooks Central Park.

A NEW PARTNER

Having learned the hard lessons of running a business, Ralph knew he still needed more talented specialists to help him run Polo. Specifically, he needed someone who knew manufacturing—how to produce clothes and ship them on time.

Ralph had met Peter Strom back in 1968, when he had first become partners with Norman Hilton. Strom had been Hilton's right-hand man. But he had left Hilton in 1974 to go into the carpet business with a friend. However, when Ralph kept calling Strom for

Peter Strom joined Polo/Ralph Lauren as the company's president at the end of 1984 so Ralph could concentrate on the creative side of the organization while Strom handled the business side. (Mark Jenkinson.)

advice, it became clear that he should go back into the garment industry, working for Polo.

Strom proved to be the best choice Ralph had made so far. He was an expert in manufacturing and knew the importance of shipping goods on time. Although others had tried, Strom was able to make Ralph adhere to shipping deadlines.

It soon became clear that Strom could handle the business side of Polo, leaving the creative side to Ralph. Soon after joining Polo, Ralph made Strom a partner by selling him ten percent of the company.

Chapter 7

Riding High in the Eighties

Polo's business improved greatly in 1975. Products were shipped, debts payed, and payments received on time. Saks Fifth Avenue had been selling Polo suits with their own store label inside, but now agreed to sell the Polo line with the Polo label.

Also, a license was sold to Hishayi, a Japanese company, to make and distribute Polo ties in Japan. In the years to come, Polo would sign many more licensing agreements, with makers of shoes, furs, lingerie, scarfs, Japanese men's wear, eye glass frames, and even Tiffany & Company, the Fifth Avenue jeweler. In 1976, Polo's sales were close to $18 million, which included sales of all licensed products.

THE LICENSING JACKPOT

During the 1970s, it became clear to fashion designers that they could become millionaires overnight through profitable licensing agreements. Licensing did not require any investment of a designer's own money or all the headaches and costs of manufacturing the clothes. It was important to control the quality of the products that went to stores with the designer's name or logo on them. But this could be done to most designers' satisfaction.

Ralph Lauren Perfume

In October of 1976, Ralph signed a licensing agreement to put his name on a line of perfume. There is a history of fashion designers putting their names on perfume bottles—Coco Channel was the first, with Channel No. 5 in the 1920s. Fashion designers believe that if wearing their clothing designs can make a person feel a certain way, so can wearing a certain scent that they help create.

Ralph had been approached by several big cosmetics and perfume companies, but he did not want to be one of many perfumes that a big company sold. He didn't want the Ralph Lauren scent to get lost in a long list of products.

A new company was formed specifically to produce and market perfumes bearing Ralph Lauren's name. The corporate giant Warner Communications provided $300,000 for start-up capital. The company was run and partly owned by two cosmetic industry executives. Ralph Lauren provided the designer name and received five percent **royalty** on all sales.

What's in a Name? Plenty!

The first perfumes sold were Polo cologne for men and Lauren perfume for women. Other scents and a line of cosmetics were added over the years. Some, however, were not successful and eventually were discontinued. In time, Warner Communications sold their share of the business to Cosmair, a French cosmetics firm.

Over all, the license has been highly successful for Ralph Lauren. It is estimated that in 1987 alone, the worldwide sales of Ralph Lauren fragrances reached about $125 million. Ralph's personal earnings from that sum were about $6.25 million. Not a bad return when one considers that he did not have to invest one penny of his own money, only his designer name.

FASHION TRENDS OF THE EIGHTIES

During the 1980s, Ralph had many successful collections and created several fashion trends. He also branched out into children's clothes. After introducing a boy's wear line in 1978, he followed with a line for girls in 1981.

In 1979, his women's wear collection had a western look, with fringed leather jackets, long prairie skirts, cowboy boots, satin cowboy shirts, Stetson hats, and glittering silver buckles.

Five big New York department stores bought the entire collection. Surprising many critics who called the clothes "costumes," the western look had great appeal to American women, even in big cities like New York. Many designers quickly imitated the idea.

During a charity affair at the Museum of American Folk Art, in New York City, Ricky and Ralph Lauren stand in front of a display depicting the early West. This was an appropriate setting for the man who has popularized the western look in men's and women's fashions. (Jack Manning/NYT Pictures.)

The New West Look

While on a trip to Santa Fe, New Mexico, with his wife and children, Ralph was again inspired to bring America's traditional designs to today's fashions for men and women.

The New West collection was introduced in 1981 and was also an immediate success. The patterns and colors were influenced by native American Indian designs of rugs, blankets, and tribal art. The collection included chamois skirts, sweaters with patterns and colors much like Navaho Indian blankets, and concha belts. The belts are made from silver pieces, originally crafted by Navaho Indians and later adapted by the Pueblo tribe.

Victorian Lace

After the New West collection, Ralph turned again to America's English and European heritage for inspiration. In addition to New West attire, the rest of his collection for the fall of 1982 was a complete fashion "about face" from the cowboy look. This trend-setting collection featured a lacy, Victorian look for women's wear, with high-necked, lace-trimmed blouses; close-fitting, hunting-style jackets; and velvet and fine wool dresses.

Ralph has said that the collection was inspired by what he calls "Old World" style. "Your grandmothers had this stuff," he has said, referring to the lace-trimmed blouses and long skirts. "But when I showed it the customers couldn't find it. Maybe they could find it in thrift shops, that was it."

Once again, Ralph's instincts for knowing what kinds of clothes customers wanted were right on target. The lacy, Old World look was a runaway hit, with many other designers later racing to catch up with Ralph Lauren's lead.

The Home Collection

In 1983, about the same time his Old World look became so popular, Ralph moved into a new area of fashion design—the Ralph Lauren Home Collection. Once again, Ralph was an innovator. This time it was fashion designs for the home. He introduced a 2,500-piece collection of household items in 1983 that were first sold in several major department stores around the country.

Much of the Ralph Lauren Home Collection carried over ideas and images of his clothing fashions—the traditional, English country house setting or the western look was now translated into home decor.

The Home Collection was licensed to the J.P. Stevens Company, known best for its linens and towels. Since Ralph insisted on introducing all 2,500 items in the line at one time, there were many problems with the early products and the marketing of the collection. In addition to delivery problems from the many factories making the merchandise, the quality of the items was often poor.

Also, Ralph once again demanded that all his home products be sold in one shop in the department stores. Although this marketing approach was successful for men's and women's wear, in the housewares area it hurt rather than helped sales.

In 1984, the license for the Home Collection was taken away from J.P. Stevens. In 1986, the line became a wholly owned subsidiary of Polo/Ralph Lauren. And by 1987, most of the Home Collection problems were ironed out and the line became very profitable.

With the Home Collection, Ralph Lauren became the first major fashion designer to offer a complete line of furniture and other home decor products. These include such items as bedding, blankets, table linens, fabrics, wall coverings, floor coverings, towels, dishes, crystal glassware, and giftware.

THE RHINELANDER MANSION

Perhaps the peak moment of Ralph's success throughout the eighties was the opening of the Polo/Ralph Lauren store in the Rhinelander Mansion. Located on 72nd Street and Madison Avenue in New York City, the Rhinelander Mansion is a five-story, limestone building. It was originally built in 1894 by the wealthy Gertrude Rhinelander, who wanted her home to look like a French chateau. The mansion took five years to build and had a ballroom, billiard parlor, and bowling alley.

The Rhinelander Mansion in New York City is without question the most prestigious of all Polo/Ralph Lauren stores. After the store opened in 1986, sales were over $30 million for the first year. (William E. Sauro/NYT Pictures.)

For Ralph's purposes, it cost over $30 million and took 1½ years to restore the building. In 1986, the mansion opened as the "palace" among the firm's stores. Within its walls many Polo/Ralph Lauren products are displayed to Ralph's exacting wishes. It is such a lavish and remarkable store that many tourists visiting New York stop in just to walk around and browse at the unusual displays.

Chapter 8

Dark Moments at the Top

It was November 1986, and a show of Ralph Lauren's fashions for the spring of 1987 had just concluded. As always, the applauding audience demanded that the designer come out from behind the curtains and take a bow. As he had done for the past fifteen years, Ralph Lauren walked down the runway and thanked the audience for their enthusiastic reception of his designs.

Yet, deep inside, Ralph wondered if this was the last fashion show he'd ever see.

A FRIGHTENING SECRET

Ralph had a frightening secret. A tumor had been growing at the base of his brain for the past nine years. Ralph had first discovered it when he had some unusual ringing in his ears. Doctors told him that the ringing was caused by a tiny, benign (noncancerous) tumor in his brain. It was a reason for concern, but not panic. There seemed to be no need to operate at the time because the tumor could remain the same, small size for Ralph's entire life.

At first, Ralph thought a lot about the tumor. Then, day by day, year by year, his worries faded away. The tumor didn't seem to bother him at all.

But in 1986, while having a routine medical checkup, Ralph's doctors found that the tumor had become much larger. When the doctors told Ralph that it was time to operate, "That was about the scariest moment of my life," he said later.

It had been a hard year for Ralph in other ways as well. His father had become very ill with heart disease and needed a serious operation. And Ralph's brother Jerry had also become quite ill that year. Because Ralph was so close to his family, these events were very disturbing for him.

Moments of Despair

The tumor was growing so slowly that Ralph was able to plan the operation eight months in advance, after he had finished his fall 1987 collection. He wanted to keep the illness a secret and only told his family and closest friends. He thought it would hurt his business severely if people believed he was facing a life-threatening illness.

Just before the operation, Ralph's picture was on the cover of *Time* magazine. But with the operation coming up, it was hard for Ralph to enjoy this moment of success. Everyone thought he was at the top of the world, the man of the hour in the fashion industry.

But secretly, Ralph knew he was facing one of the most critical moments of his life. Doctors could make educated guesses, but there were no guarantees. The tumor could be cancerous, or it could cause other severe medical problems. There was also no guarantee that Ralph would survive the operation unimpaired.

Ralph had some frightening and lonely thoughts at this time. But, as he said later, the threat to his life gave him a deeper appreciation of all the good times and good fortune he had enjoyed.

A Successful Operation

The operation was performed on April 13, 1987. It lasted 5½ hours and was a success. Ralph and his family were delighted, but he was a restless patient. Less than a week after the surgery, he walked out of the hospital.

Ralph took a few months off from work to recover. He rested in his home at Montauk Point, a 5½-acre oceanfront estate at the farthest tip of Long Island. After Montauk, he traveled with his family to the 12,300-acre ranch that he owns in Colorado.

While Ralph was away from the garment center hubbub, rumors circulated throughout the industry that he was deathly ill. Of course, it wasn't true. By August, Ralph was able to return to his office, begin designing upcoming collections, and show the world he was back, better than ever.

ANSWERING CRITICS

Although Ralph is undoubtedly one of the most successful American designers of all time, he still has critics in the fashion design industry. They will argue that Ralph is not really a designer because he has none of the formal training most designers acquire at schools

Ralph Lauren and his creative advertising team work in a relaxed, outdoor setting near his home at Montauk Point, on New York's Long Island. (Dirck Halstead/Time Magazine.)

or by working in apprentice positions at design houses. He does not know how to sketch, drape and cut fabric, or cut patterns. Nor does he have any of the many other basic technical skills that one needs in the step-by-step process of making clothes.

Some wonder how Ralph can call himself a designer at all. They say that he's really just a genius at marketing clothes, or that he copies other styles and merely changes or adapts them.

Ralph has never denied his lack of design school training. He argues against his critics by saying that he is always able to hire skilled stylists, tailors, and other technicians. However, the creative visions for his collections are all from his own imagination.

An entire list of products sold with a Ralph Lauren or Polo label would presently number over 110,000 items. They include clothes for men, women, and children as well as accessories, fragrances, home furnishings, and housewares. Ralph insists that he personally works on each article that is sold with a Ralph Lauren or Polo label. "I do it," he has said. "It's not done for me. I'm not an overseer."

It's true that Ralph is also a genius at marketing and promoting his products. He has clearly revolutionized the way big department stores present and sell clothes to customers. The Polo/Ralph Lauren label has maintained a reputation with shoppers for high quality and exclusivity.

A RICH, SELF-MADE MAN

Ralph Lauren's personal fortune is now estimated at about $600 million dollars. In addition to his New York apartment on Fifth Avenue, the Montauk home, and the Colorado ranch, Ralph also owns a 200-acre estate in Westchester County, a wealthy area north of Manhattan, and a villa in Jamaica. His collection of miniature, classic cars in his office is matched by a collection of full-sized, antique cars. And when his travel needs demand more speed than an antique car can offer, he might take off in his own Gulfstream II jet airplane.

As one of the country's richest, self-made men, the boy from the Bronx has achieved his childhood dream of becoming a millionaire hundreds of times over. He has also greatly influenced how people shop, dress, and decorate their homes in America and around the world.

Glossary

bankruptcy A legal declaration of an inability to pay debts.

boutique A small specialty shop.

buyer A person who buys goods for a retail store or manufacturer.

capital Money or goods that can be used to produce an income.

collateral Something of value that is pledged to guarantee repayment of a loan.

draping A skill used in designing clothing which involves shaping and pinning fabric (usually muslin, a thin cotton gauze) on a model in order to achieve the proper design and fit of a garment.

entrepreneur A person who organizes, controls, and takes all the risks of running a business.

fabric houses Companies that manufacture fabrics primarily for the makers of clothing and home products.

factor A financial organization that loans money to businesses on the basis of goods that have been shipped or orders that have been received.

financial backer A person who or an organization that provides money for business ventures.

fitting model A special model who works with pattern makers to determine the proper proportions and fit of a garment.

Great Depression A period during the 1930s of low economic activity in the United States, with much unemployment.

licensing agreement A contract that grants the use of a name (or many types of original materials) for a fee or royalty.

line A single category of merchandise produced by a manufacturer having several different styles and sizes, such as a line of cars or a line of dresses.

logo A name, symbol, or other device for identifying a product or company name; usually registered with the government as a trademark and therefore can only be used by the owner of such registration.

marketing Sales strategies used to appeal to potential buyers of a product or service.

61

merchandise   Goods that are bought or sold.

pattern making   The cutting of separate pieces of fabric of various shapes from a solid cloth and then sewing them together.

retail   The sale of goods to the general public.

royalty   An amount of money paid by an organization that has the right (license) to use or sell a work (book, piece of music, play, etc.), name (trademark), or product that is owned by an individual or another organization.

stock   The supply or inventory of goods on hand.

trademark   A unique name, feature, or symbol associated with a particular product.

Index